I Did not Learn This at NP School

A Practical Guide to Starting Your Own Nurse Practitioner Practice

Dr. Priscilla Naamomo Otubuah,
PhD, DNP, FNP-BC, PMHNP-BC

DORRANCE
PUBLISHING CO
EST. 1920
PITTSBURGH, PENNSYLVANIA 15238

Dorrance Publishing Co
585 Alpha Drive
Suite 103
Pittsburgh, PA 15238
Visit our website at *www.dorrancebookstore.com*

ISBN: 979-8-8860-4671-7
eISBN: 979-8-8860-4755-4

To God be the glory for the great things He has done.

I dedicate this book to my lovely and amazing husband,

Akrofi Otubuah.

Thank you for loving me, believing in me,

and supporting me in every capacity.

To our awesome son,

Nii Kunim Kabu Otubuah;

you are a shining star.

Acknowledgment

I acknowledge all the hardworking nurses and nurse practitioners out there! You are all healthcare heroes. Thank you to all my nursing instructors from my Associate's Degree in Nursing (ADN) to Doctor of Philosophy in Nursing (Ph.D.), especially Dr. Aurelia Macabasco-O'Connell, Ph.D.; you once told me that I am a "mover and a shaker" and that has propelled me to higher heights in my career.

Contents

Chapter One

Why Did I Become a Nurse?

Why did you become a nurse? This is a question that every nurse has answered at one point in their nursing education or career. Most instructors would start a class by asking each student why they decided to become a nurse. It is amazing how one always seems to learn something different while appreciating the diverse perspective why people chose this career path. Some have trodden this route because they knew from a young age that they wanted to become nurses, while some attribute the passion and desire from family members (whose relatives were nurses or encountered an amazing nurse in caring for themselves or a family member), and others have related their choice to a particular incident that changed the course of their lives. I wait in anticipation to hear the drive, passion, and decision of why different people decided to become nurses.

Whenever this question is asked, I pause and internally reflect before I provide an answer. Unlike some people who knew at a tender age that they wanted to become nurses, I was not in that category. I always dreamt of becoming a lawyer and defending the innocent in my quest for justice for all. I also saw myself as a successful journalist who was on prime television reading the news or interviewing influential people. Right from elementary school, I was interested in arts and history. I loved to read and write and was fascinated about world history and government. Hence, I spent a great deal of time reading about Shakespeare, writing my own imaginary stories/poems, and learning about ancient Egypt and the medieval times. I even went on to become a radio presenter on an evening gospel music show in my late teenage years in Ghana, West Africa. I appreciate Elder Karl Morris-Dubgartey for giving me the great opportunity to be on air. Soon after marriage, I migrated to the United States of America and my outlook on nursing changed. I saw strong and dedicated people skillfully providing quality patient care with joy and passion.

My husband was instrumental in my decision to become a nurse and I am eternally grateful to him. He encouraged me and supported me in every step of the way. He worked long hours so he could afford my tuition. I had no background experience as a nurse and I started off my nursing education at a community college. My first clinical rotation was intimidating. I encountered some nurses who have practiced nursing for many years and some were mean and rude to me. I felt sad and even wondered if nursing was the right field for me. Nevertheless, there was an inner passion that pushed me to look beyond the unfriendly and discourteous treatment from these veteran nurses. I vowed on that first day that I would become a better nurse, and I will be generous and patient to any new nurse that I have the privilege of mentoring or precepting. After many years of practicing nursing, I continue to uphold this principle. I started a certified nursing assistant school and joyfully trained the students to become the best nursing assistants. I have volunteered in numerous health fairs as a Nurse Practitioner and I continue to precept NP students from different schools across the United States of America.

I graduated with an Associate's Degree in Nursing (ADN). I then went on to obtain a Bachelor's Degree in Nursing (BSN), Master of Science in Nursing (MSN), a post-masters in Nursing, a Doctor of Nursing Practice and finally a Doctor of Philosophy in Nursing (Ph.D.). The journey was not easy; it demanded a lot of sacrifice, hard work, and dedication. There were times that I cried and felt discouraged. Nevertheless, I was determined to become a highly skilled and efficient nurse leader. Although I did not become a lawyer, I am able to advocate for patients in my role as a nurse and more so as a Nurse Practitioner. Additionally, as an NP business owner, I am able to deliberate on a higher managerial role and advocate for patients on a different platform.

In my book entitled *Can You Handle This Dream*, I shared how "In the early years of my nursing career, I was floated to different units in the hospital where I worked at. I was initially a pediatric registered nurse but I ended up on the adult medical surgical unit, telemetry, post-anesthesia care unit, emergency room, you name it. I became a relief charge nurse and assisted in many administrative roles. I did not understand the process and I got frustrated at some point. Little did I know that, the experiences on the different units and the managerial skills were preparing me for an exciting career later on in life where all the learned skills and experience would matter and, become profitable" (Otubuah, pp. 25-26, 2022).

You do not need to float to all the different units at the hospital or at your place of work in order to have an experience worth preparing you for your role as an NP or as a NP business owner. You might have worked on only one unit but are you faithful and diligent in discharging your RN duties? Are you a prudent nurse or an incompetent nurse? Even when you are floated to different units, are you always complaining and unproductive? Check your attitude and make a conscious decision to learn something new every day. Let your RN experiences be worth your time.

Know your strengths and weaknesses. When you are not skillful or competent in a particular area, invest time to study and know more. There are many relevant continuing education units (CEUs) out there that can help you to enrich your nursing knowledge and practice. Remember that you are always going to be a Registered Nurse even when you become a Nurse Practitioner. Most states require you to maintain an active RN license while you practice as an NP. Build a strong RN foundation that you can build a monumental NP career on. As you come to the end of this chapter, I want you to spend some time to reflect on and complete this exercise on why you became a nurse in the first place. Be truthful and honest as you complete this step.

Notes
Take Time to Reflect On: Why did I become a nurse?

Chapter Two

Are You Satisfied with Your Current Position?

Most people ask me such questions as: Why do you have so many degrees in nursing? Why didn't you just obtain a Ph.D.? Why did you obtain a DNP? Why did you become a Family Nurse Practitioner (FNP) and then go on to become a Psychiatric Mental Health Nurse Practitioner (PMHNP)? And the questions are endless. My answer to them is simple: I am driven by excellence, service, and passion. I am blessed with a supportive husband and family. Hence my dreams became a reality. You do not have to attain all these degrees if you do not have the tenacity, resilience, and resources. Find out what you are passionate about and dedicate time to pursue it. At the end of the day, find out what works best for you and enjoy doing it.

My humble question to you is: Are you happy with your current nursing position? If not, then reevaluate yourself and make some life-defining decisions. Maybe you have an Associate's Degree and you are contemplating on going back to school. Sit down and count the cost. Make sure that you have done a good assessment, diagnosis, planning, implementation, and evaluation (ADPIE). As an experienced RN, you have used the ADPIE process throughout your nursing career. This is the time for you to sit back and personalize the process for your good, even in your quest for higher learning. Take time to decide and plan on the following essential building blocks:

- What are your short-term goals?
- What are your long-term goals?
- What are the means to achieving the goals?
- What are the potential barriers that you anticipate to face?
- How are you going to overcome the barriers?

There are many Registered Nurses (RNs) who go back to school to become Nurse Practitioners (NPs) only to realize that they prefer to practice as RNs and not as NPs. Some of these choices are based on personal decisions and some are based on financial decisions. Soon after graduation, some new graduate NPs realize that they are spending more time seeing more patients and earning less than they did when they were RNs. Some are also halted in their decision to become primary care providers and taking on more patient responsibilities unlike the former, when they took orders and carried out the instructions of practitioners or medical doctors. Best practice is to do the background work before investing into a big undertaking and making a major career change.

As you make a decision to become an NP, here is a list of some of the NP specialties out there. The world is evolving and the nursing world is no exception. Stay up to date with what is new even in the NP world. I urge you to take the time and learn about the specific primary duties of each of these specialties:

- Clinical Nurse Specialist (CNS)
- Certified Nurse Midwife (CNM)
- Certified Registered Nurse Anesthetist (CRNA)
- Acute Care Nurse Practitioner (ACNP)
- Emergency Nurse Practitioner (ENP)
- Adult-Gerontology Nurse Practitioner (AGNP)
- Family Nurse Practitioner (FNP)
- Neonatal Nurse Practitioner (NNP)
- Pediatric Nurse Practitioner (PNP)
- Psychiatric Mental Health Nurse Practitioner (PMHNP)
- Women's Health Nurse Practitioner (WHNP)
- Orthopedic Nurse Practitioner (ONP)
- Hospice Nurse Practitioner (HNP)
- Dermatology Certified Nurse Practitioner (DCNP)
- Cardiac Nurse Practitioner (CNP)
- Surgical Nurse Practitioner (SNP)
- Holistic Care Nurse Practitioner (HCNP)

As a professional, know what the intricacies of the profession are. For instance, it behooves one to know what the complete job requirements are; you will also need to know what the average salary for NPs are. After deciding on what specialty that you want to focus on, take the time to investigate what the requirements for school admissions are. Do your research on the best accredited school for your specialty. Do not settle for comfort at the expense of quality education. You do not want to spend a reasonable amount of time in school, graduate, and then realize that the school was not accredited. Basically, most places of employment will not hire you and you might not even be able to take the certifying board examination. Be wise, be smart and maximize all the resources available to you. No man or woman is an island. Interact with people who are already ahead of you and are successful at what they are doing. Do not waste time in your pursuit for higher learning and excellence.

Then there is a decision to either obtain a Doctor of Nursing Practice (DNP) or a Doctor of Philosophy in Nursing (Ph.D.) or both. The first question I ask people in this kind of dilemma is what their passion is. Simply put, the DNP degree is a practice or clinical doctorate whereas the Ph.D. is primarily a research doctorate. Another major difference between the two is the amount of time it takes for completion. The DNP takes a shorter time as compared to the Ph.D.

A word of advice I always give to Doctoral students is to maximize their time and accomplish their educational goals within specified times. This can be done by deciding very early in the program on what research topic and on what kind of research methodology (qualitative, quantitative, descriptive, exploratory, etc.) one wants to embark on. This saves you time and you are able to focus on your particular topic with every class that you take. You can then start doing the research, literature review, and gathering as much information as you can in preparation for your final dissertation.

My DNP project focused on the effectiveness of health coaching on improving self-monitoring and medication adherence among African-Americans with hypertension. The results from the project showed that a health coach can help the African-American patient with hypertension to attain a positive change in blood pressure management. Also, the health beliefs and medication adherence of the participants were positively influenced by the health coaching intervention. With my Ph.D. research, I decided to do an in-depth study by looking at the effects of health coaching on self-care monitoring among Ghanaians with hypertension living in Southern California. The results of the study showed significant improvements in the health beliefs and medication adherence of the participants. Again, the health coaching intervention was effective in the management of hypertension among Ghanaians.

I enjoyed doing both research and the perspectives I derived from a DNP perspective and a Ph.D. perspective are educational pearls that I will uphold throughout my life. My initial plan was to go to Ghana and implement the health coaching intervention at a marketplace. Due to the COVID-19 pandemic, I could not travel to Ghana but by the advice and counsel of my able committee chair I was able to decide on doing the intervention at a predominantly Ghanaian church in Southern California. You have to be wise, flexible, teachable, and willing to make quick adjustments in your educational pursuit.

Do not waste time trying to figure out something that is impossible when you have all the possibilities in front of you. Utilize the resources you have and know what works and use it to your advantage. There are people who take too much time to complete a doctoral degree and it is as a result of a myriad of reasons. Some of these reasons could be personal, family, financial, health, and many other factors. In as much as your reasons are genuine, your challenges and problems cannot stop the hands of time. The seconds, minutes, hours, days, weeks, months, and years are set in motion and they will continue to move on, even when you are inactive. Do what is best for you but at the same time be disciplined, resilient, and focused.

Know when to take a break, when to pause, and when to keep on going. You might not graduate with your cohort but you can make a decision to join another graduating class. You went to school to finish and graduate so accomplish that goal. Your school commencement is proof of your tenacity and quest for success. At the end of the day, the onus falls on you to dream, persevere, and attain your goals in life. I ask you the question again; are you satisfied, and I mean really satisfied with your current job requirements and duties? Give yourself a fair rating and then intervene accordingly.

Notes
Take Time to Reflect On:
What is the current level of my job satisfaction?

Chapter Three

I Want to Start My Own NP Business; What Is the First Step?

So now you are convinced that you want to start your own Nurse Practitioner Practice. That is good but there is more to starting your own practice or business than a passionate desire. Let us talk about first things first. Based on your specialty, you have to decide on what kind of practice you want to start. Is it going to be:

- Family Medicine
- Mental Health
- Pediatrics
- Neonatology
- Oncology
- Emergency Medicine
- Geriatrics
- Addiction Medicine
- Hospice and Palliative Medicine

- Occupational Health Nursing
- Psychosomatic Medicine

Next, know what the state laws and regulations are (discussed in Chapter 4). Will it be a remote practice or do you need an office space? As a general rule, start small and then build on what you have started. In your strategic planning, utilize the strengths, weaknesses, opportunities, and threats analysis (SWOT) to determine the location and needs in the area you want to start the practice. Be able to identify some opportunities and some potential threats you might encounter. Write up a business plan. Count the cost and then implement your plans. These steps seem simple but you have to be meticulous and detailed. There are no shortcuts. Invest time and energy for the realization of your dreams because the successful completion of one stage will prepare you to advance to the next stage.

There are different kinds of business plans out there. Again, I encourage you to research and focus on what your particular interest is. You do not have to follow verbatim every step listed here; this a practical guide and experiences that helped me in my business setup. You can improvise and make changes based on what your unique needs are. Let us take a look at some of the elements of a sample business plan.

- Executive Summary
- General Company Description (mission statement; practice goals and objectives; business philosophy; legal form of ownership)
- Legal Environment (licensing; special regulations; payments)
- Management and Organizations (manager (s))

- Owners/Operators
- History and Information
- Personnel Plan/Salaries
- Industry Overview
- Market Needs
- Competition
- Competition Advantage
- Location
- Demographics of the Location
- Marketing Strategies
- Professional and Advisory Support
- Financial Information
- Projected First-Year Income
- Expenses (all opening expenses and improvements)
- Other Details

Now that you have the basics in place, you have to decide on what type of business structure your setup is going to be. The Internal Revenue Service (IRS) posits that the most common forms of business are sole proprietorship, partnership, corporation, and S corporation. A Limited Liability Company (LLC) is allowed by state statute. Below is a list of business structures per the IRS:

- Sole Proprietorship
- Partnership
- Corporations
- S Corporations
- Limited Liability Company (LLC)

Please visit the IRS website to learn the details of each business structure. Research on the business taxes and stay current with the small business publications and other meaningful resources. You will need an Employer Identification Number (EIN), National Provider Identifier (NPI) for individual providers, and group practice NPI. Additionally, make sure you have an active license, board certification, and the U.S. Drug Enforcement Agency (DEA) number. Familiarize yourself with the cost and process for obtaining a license, certification (based on your specialty), and a DEA. Register with the Council for Affordable Quality Healthcare (CAQH) ProView for providers and keep your information current per requirements.

As mentioned in previous chapters, you need to keep an active license as a Registered Nurse and also an active license as a Nurse Practitioner (based on your specialty). Determine to complete your board certification as well (most insurance companies will only contract with a board-certified practitioner). In the U.S., any provider who intends to prescribe legal controlled substances must register with the DEA (contact the DEA directly on pricing and the steps to take). Upon registration, you are assigned a number to include on any controlled substances that you prescribe (Schedule II-V drugs). This helps the DEA to track controlled substances transactions. Visit the DEA website to learn about obtaining a DEA and the legal requirements as designated.

Notes
Take Time to Reflect On:
What are the steps to starting my own practice?

Chapter Four

Knowing the Laws, Regulations, and Requirements

Every state is different so take the time to know your state laws, regulations, and requirements as well as those of the other states that you can potentially practice in. Each state has a different scope of practice for Advanced Practice Registered Nurses (APRNs). Although some states grant APRNs the authority to practice fully, other states require APRNs to practice under the supervision of a Medical Doctor (MD). According to the American Association of Nurse Practitioners (AANP) there are 26 states, D.C., and two U.S. territories with full practice authority (AANP, 2022).

Further, familiarize yourself with the various ways of providing patient care. The traditional in-person office visits have specific laws and regulations that govern the day-to-day operations. Additionally, telehealth has gradually become a mainstay in healthcare. As patients become comfortable on the virtual platforms and lawmakers deliberate on safe, efficient, and HIPAA compliant means of delivery and communication, more NPs will have the privilege of attending to a wider patient population. Do not be caught unawares in the legalities of healthcare. Ignorance is not an excuse in healthcare since the lives of patients are sometimes directly or indirectly impacted by what you do or by what you omit. Know what you can do and what you cannot do as an NP in any state that you are licensed to practice in. There are many resources out there for you to utilize to your benefit. Always start with your board of nursing.

Further, it will be of a great benefit to you to get legal services and advise. Get an expert in healthcare laws based on the state that you want to practice in. Shop around and ask the right questions. Spend the money and time to get the factual legal advice you need for your particular practice. It is not enough to only go by what other people tell you based on their experiences and what is working for them. Your unique need and situation might be different. What another person might tell you may not be accurate based on a myriad of factors, circumstances, and changes in an evolving healthcare system.

One of the good things about the structure of the American health system is that there are defined lists of protocols and guidelines that works. Such information is readily available on demand in various ways and on different platforms. One must, however, be cautious when accessing legal information and requirements. It is always best to go to the original source for information. Inasmuch social media and other electronic platforms are simply available to anyone who searches for it, one must be mindful of the fact that there is fake news and inaccurate information that appears real. Do not take everything on face value. After all, you are, or you will soon become, a business owner. It behooves on you to investigate from a reliable source before you make an informed decision.

Your decision can cause you loss of money, time, and increased stress. This can easily be avoided if one is willing to pause, reflect, and then act. In preparing for your own NP practice, it is imperative and of paramount importance that you are well informed and up-to-date on the laws, regulations, and requirements per your special practice needs.

Notes

Take Time to Reflect On: What are the laws, regulations, and requirements in my state?

Chapter Five

Do You Have the Money, Time and Resources?

As discussed in Chapter 3, you have to count the cost before you start the NP practice that you have always dreamed about. The practice is not only going to function on your awesome and amazing ideas and big dreams. As with every working engine, one needs the right oil to lubricate the parts for the machinery to work and to continue to work well. It is not a secret that you will need money, time, and resources in order to have a successful practice. All your great ideas are meaningless without the monetary vehicle and other essential parts to make your dreams a reality. You need to have an effective fiscal machinery and mechanism in place at your anticipated NP practice.

I advise Nurse Practitioners (NPs) not to quit their NP job because they are excited to start an NP practice. Starting your own practice is a great venture that is going to require a lot of financial input before you begin to see any meaningful output. I am by no means advocating for you to overwork yourself. Unless you have (1) saved thousands of dollars, (2) just inherited a lot of money, or (3) have a miraculous and unlimited flow of cash for the next five years or more. Know that you are going to need finances to run the practice. You do not have to overdo it and kill yourself with working too many hours.

Moreover, the practice will also suffer because you will not have the time, joy, and capacity to manage the business aspect of your practice when you are overworking as an NP. Regardless, you need to have a balance work life. There is no magic formula to starting a successful practice. You are going to need good planning, sacrifice, time, and money before you can confidently see productivity and growth. A tree, they say, does not grow overnight. It needs the right nutrients, sunlight, time, and other necessary conditions for growth. Likewise, you have a beautiful idea to start a business but it will take time for that beauty to be evident.

In fact, the initial stages might not look beautiful at all. Some people might think you are just a dreamer and that you are not in touch with reality. You will be mocked at, laughed at, and even be ignored by some people. You might get frustrated at a point in time, you might have some doubts, and you might even cry at one point. Sometimes, the trails and frustrations are meant to give you inner strength to become resilient and prepare you for the potential challenges and hurdles that you might have to overcome to attain to your dreams. Some of the friends and people you trust might not understand your vision so they will not understand your purpose and what you stand for. Do not waste your time trying to explain yourself a million times to a million people.

The hard truth is that the right people meant to help you will be there for you and will stay by your side no matter how high the ocean of frustration arise. On the other hand, do not put all your confidence, hope, and trust in people to help you. This is because you will get deeply hurt, offended, and sometimes become stagnant if those people disappoint you. This is your dream and not necessarily the dream of the people you are looking up to. Be strong, tenacious, and yet flexible enough to adapt to change at any given point in time.

I will be doing a disservice to you if I do not tell you the truth, that most people will not believe in your dream and some people will simply discourage you. For all you know, some of the people you confide in might have had an idea or might have even attempted to start an NP practice but were unsuccessful. The fact that they did not succeed is not a guarantee that you will not succeed as well. Learn from their mistakes and avoid those mistakes that they made in your own NP practice setup. You might attract hostility, intimidation, and jealousy; some situations might even land you in isolation. Be a strong a person both on the inside and on the outside. Do not let people take you for granted. Know your worth and do not settle for less. After all, you are smart enough to have completed RN school and even go on to become an NP. You did not give up in your beginning stages, why are you now getting discouraged?

As I mentioned previously, I did not have an initial interest in science. I enjoyed arts and my early years of school was focused on such study areas as English, literature, and social studies. When I started the prerequisites for nursing school, I went through all my English and humanities courses at the community college with ease. Then I had to concentrate on the sciences. Such science courses as chemistry, physics, microbiology, anatomy, and physiology were dreaded subjects that did not initially excite me. Nevertheless, I immediately realized that I would have to take these subjects before I could proceed to nursing school. No nursing school was going to accept me into their nursing program because I excelled in the arts. I studied a lot and put a lot of time to learn the subjects and topics per requirements. I was not just interested in passing a class and getting a good grade. I made up my mind to understand the scientific basis and underpinnings of health and illness.

This solid foundation has guided me throughout my nursing and NP careers. Regardless of your background, you also had to academically endure a lot to get to where you currently are. Starting your NP practice is another stage in your life and you need a sturdy and firm approach to overcome this stage as well. In fact, you might not have learned any practical steps to starting your own NP practice at school so I understand your nervousness and anticipation. Be encouraged that when there is a will there is a way. You have the will to start this NP practice so keep that hope alive and strive to win the victory. Before I end this chapter, I want to emphasize on these three essential blocks again, thus money, time, and resource.

Money
- Do you have enough cash flow to start and sustain the practice?
- Do you have a good credit to obtain a loan?
- Can you even afford a loan?
- How are you going to finance the practice?

Time
- How many hours a day/week are you going to commit to the practice?
- How long is it going to take you to get all the initial structures in place?
- How long is it going to take for the practice to get approval from licensing agents, contractors, insurance companies, and many others?

Resource

- What specific resources would you need in order to start your practice?
- Do you have readily available resources to start and sustain your NP practice?
- How are you going to have access to these resources?

Notes

Take Time to Reflect On: Do I have the money, time and resources?

Chapter Six

Congratulations on Starting Your Own NP Practice

I want to personally congratulate you and welcome you to your new NP practice. It might have taken you months or even years to get here but you have arrived despite the opposition and challenges. You have all your ducks in a row and you are now ready to open the doors to patient care. But is this really the end? Of course not! The journey to starting your own NP practice has just begun. Be proud of yourself because you have accomplished a great feat. Your family, friends, and the entire world are about to hear about your awesome practice and the amazing and excellent patient care you will be providing to patients and their families.

You will never forget that first patient that walks through your door. You will never forget that insurance company that approved your credentialing and gave you the first contract, and you will not forget the first patient that files a grievance against your NP practice. These are memories that you will keep for many years to come. Some memories are good and some are bad. Even though you might not be able to control all the variables that make up the memories, you can create a conducive and serene practice environment that will help create and foster positive memories. You have gathered documents and information to arrive at this stage. I want to remind you to keep hard and electronic copies of all these documents. Have a system in place to remind you of expiration dates on licenses, insurances, and certificates. Have the following documents readily accessible for yourself and the practice.

For Yourself
- Copy of RN/NP license
- Board Certification(s)
- BLS, ACLS, and other disciplines
- Certificate of Insurance
- CAQH number
- NPI number
- PTAN/Medicare numbers
- Curriculum Vitae (CV)
- Others

Your Practice
- Business license
- Insurance license
- Articles of incorporation
- Statement of Information
- Credentialing contracts
- Taxes
- Others

Do not stop learning because you are now a business owner. If you want to continue practicing, then keep up to date with all your licensing and certification requirements. Make sure your business licenses, tax filings, and other practical and legal requirements are current.

I want to now dedicate these last pages to you to go ahead and start writing down the steps and journey to owning your own NP practice. This is not a storybook. This is a practical book so stop wishing and start working. Write your vision down and then get to work on it. Give yourself about six weeks to come up with a realistic business strategy. Each week, be sure to accomplish something meaningful. This is your workbook.

WEEK ONE

WEEK TWO

WEEK THREE

WEEK FOUR

WEEK FIVE

WEEK SIX

Reference

Otubuah, P. 2022. Can you handle this dream? Trilogy Christian Publishing.